HAPPILY EVER CRAFTER

ONCE UPON A
MEDIEVAL
CRAFT

ANNALEES LIM

Lerner Publications ◆ Minneapolis

First American edition published in 2020 by Lerner Publishing Group, Inc.

First published in Great Britain in 2018 by Wayland
Copyright © Hodder and Stoughton, 2018
All rights reserved.

Senior Commissioning Editor: Melanie Palmer
Design: Square and Circus
Illustrations: Supriya Sahai

Additional illustrations: Freepik

Lerner Publications Company
A division of Lerner Publishing Group, Inc.
241 First Avenue North
Minneapolis, MN 55401 USA

For reading levels and more information, look up this title at www.lernerbooks.com.

Main body text set in Billy Infant Regular 17/24.
Typeface provided by SparkyType.

Library of Congress Cataloging-in-Publication Data

Names: Lim, Annalees, author. | Sahai, Supriya, 1977– illustrator.
Title: Once upon a medieval craft / Annalees Lim, Supriya Sahai, [illustrator].
Description: Minneapolis : Lerner Publications, [2018] | Series: Happily ever crafter | Audience: Ages 7–11. | Audience: Grades 4–6.
Identifiers: LCCN 2018050610 (print) | LCCN 2018058682 (ebook) | ISBN 9781541561960 (eb pdf) | ISBN 9781541558793 (hb) | ISBN 9781526307545 (pb)
Subjects: LCSH: Handicraft—Juvenile literature. | Castles in art—Juvenile literature. | Handicraft for children. | Civilization, Medieval, in art—Juvenile literature. | Games—Juvenile literature. | Children's parties—Juvenile literature.
Classification: LCC TT160 (ebook) | LCC TT160 .L485246 2019 (print) | DDC 745.5—dc23

LC record available at https://lccn.loc.gov/2018050610

Manufactured in the United States of America
1-46268-46260-11/14/2018

SAFETY INFORMATION: Please ask an adult for help with any activities that could be tricky or involve cooking or handling glass. Ask adult permission when appropriate.

CONTENTS

KNIGHTS AND CASTLES

Heroic knights were a common sight between the 5th and 15th centuries, a period of time in Europe known as the Middle Ages. As new kingdoms formed, royal families would grant knighthoods to people wishing to serve as warriors. They pledged to protect and defend the monarchy and the religion they believed in.

To become a knight you had to be a great horse rider, have excellent sword wielding skills, and most importantly you had to be rich enough to buy your own armor, weapons, and horse. But don't worry—you can easily become a knight without having to trade in your treasures. In this book you will find simple crafts and party ideas made from recycled materials and things you find around the house. It won't be long before you have all the things you need to go out and complete your medieval quests.

The legend of King Arthur is probably one of the most famous stories about this period of time, but it is unknown if Arthur was a real person or not. Tales of his reign have been told many different times over the centuries. The stories all include his wife Guinevere, Merlin the Wizard, his sword Excalibur, and the Knights of the Round Table.

FACT!
The tale of George and the Dragon is so famous that England, Portugal, Georgia, Lithuania, and Greece all made him their patron saint.

FACT!
Many believe the word knight means a person who is brave, but it actually comes from an old English word for servant.

TOP TIP
Recycling and reusing unwanted things is a great way to make your craft project environmentally friendly. Always wash old food containers or fabric before you use them. Don't forget to ask an adult before you take anything you see lying around the house—it might not be ready to be recycled just yet!

KINGDOM OF COSTUMES

Dressing up in a costume is a great way to feel like you have traveled back to a different time. Medieval clothes are very different from today's fashion, but it's easy to recreate them with these simple costume ideas.

KNIGHT'S ARMOR

Knights would wear armor made from iron or steel—which means it was really heavy—to protect them from swords and spears. Try this helmet on for size. It is made from lightweight materials and will make you look the part too.

You Will Need:
- LARGE PLATE • PENCIL • SCISSORS
- CARDBOARD OR THICK CARDSTOCK
- TAPE • PAINT • PAINTBRUSH

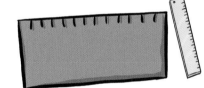

1. Draw around a plate onto some cardboard and cut the circle out.

2. Cut out a long piece of cardboard that is at least 12 inches tall and long enough to wrap around the cardboard circle. Cut slits into the top.

3. Cut out a hole from the middle of the cardboard and fold the slits down.

4. Tape the long piece of cardboard onto the circle. Cut out and add a cardboard diamond to the top.

5. Paint gray and add details in black.

PRINCESS CONE HAT

These tall headdresses, called hennins, were worn by royalty and rich people of the time. Most were about 1 ½ feet tall, but some were even taller at around 2 ½ feet. They were traditionally made from a wire mesh covered in a light fabric, but this craft can be made from recycled cardstock and tissue paper.

You Will Need:
- CARDSTOCK (YOU CAN TAPE LOTS OF PIECES TOGETHER TO MAKE IT BIG ENOUGH) • RULER • SCISSORS
- PENCIL • PAINT • PAINTBRUSH • HOLE PUNCH • TAPE
- STRING OR RIBBON • TISSUE PAPER

1. Cut out a quarter circle shape from the cardstock. The length of the straight edges will be how tall the hat will be.

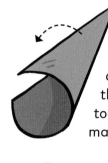

2. Wrap it around and tape the edges together to make a cone.

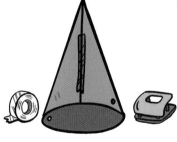

3. Punch a hole on either side of the bottom of the cone.

TOP TIP
If you don't have tissue paper, cut up strips of white or clear plastic bags and stick them to the top of the cone instead.

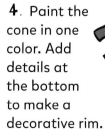

4. Paint the cone in one color. Add details at the bottom to make a decorative rim.

5. When it is dry, thread some string or ribbon into the holes. Add strips of tissue paper to the top of the cone.

SHIELD

Shields came in different shapes, and the way they were decorated showed which army or side the knight belonged to. This was useful in battle. Shields were worn on the arm and helped protect knights during attacks.

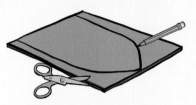

You Will Need:
- CARDBOARD • PENCIL • SCISSORS
- TAPE • WHITE CRAFT GLUE • PAINT
- PAINTBRUSH • SCRAP PAPER

1. Draw a shield shape onto the cardboard and cut it out.

2. Cut two strips of cardboard and stick them onto the back with tape.

3. Decorate the shield with the scrap pieces of cardboard and stick them in place with craft glue.

4. Paint the shield in lots of colors and leave to dry.

5. Dip the brush in a dark colored paint and wipe most of it off onto some scrap paper. Lightly paint over the shield to make it look worn from battle. This technique is called dry brushing.

DID YOU KNOW?

A round shield is called a buckler, a teardrop-shaped shield is called a kite, and the one in this craft is called a heater.

BOW AND ARROW

Archers used bows and arrows to fight in battle or to hunt animals, but today we use them mainly to shoot at targets in archery.

You Will Need:

- WIRE COAT HANGER • STRING
- MASKING TAPE • PAINT
- PAINTBRUSH • CARDSTOCK
- SCISSORS • WHITE CRAFT GLUE
- WOODEN SKEWERS

1. Bend a wire coat hanger into a curve. If an adult has wire cutters, ask them to remove the hook, but this is not necessary.

2. Tie some string to the wire. Wrap masking tape around the hanger so that it makes a solid shape.

3. Paint the bow and leave to dry.

TOP TIP

You can also make this craft using any curved sticks you find when you are out walking in a park. Use straight sticks you find for the arrows.

4. Cut out four feather shapes and two triangle shapes from colored cardstock.

5. Fold the feather shapes before sticking them onto two sides of one end of the wooden skewer. Then glue the triangles on to cover the other end.

KING OF THE CASTLE

Make your party the best celebration in the land by planning it all to perfection. You'll find all you need to entertain your fellow adventurous knights and merry maidens and create your very own medieval world with decoration ideas, themed craft projects, and more.

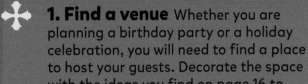

1. Find a venue Whether you are planning a birthday party or a holiday celebration, you will need to find a place to host your guests. Decorate the space with the ideas you find on page 16 to create your own themed kingdom.

2. Joking Around Jesters were a traditional way to keep guests happy, but you won't need to hire anyone to entertain the people at your party. Use the game ideas on page 12 to keep the fun going for hours.

3. Fantastic Feasts Banquets were common in medieval times, with lots of food and drink served on long tables. There are lots of simple recipes on page 20 that are so delicious that your guests will be piling their plates with goodies.

4. Perfect Presents Make prizes for the games you play, extra decorations for your themed room, or presents for your guests to thank them for coming to your party. Turn to page 24 for lots of ideas.

5. Medieval Materials Write a list of everything you need. A lot of the craft projects in this book can be made from recycled materials. Save scrap paper, old food containers, and other things you were going to throw away. Thinking creatively will save you money, and you will help to save the planet too.

GET STARTED
Don't run out of time to make all the things you need for your party. Making a list is a really easy and quick way to help you remember all the important things you need to do.

HEAR YE, HEAR YE!

Town criers used to read from scrolls to shout announcements to the public, spreading important news. Making these scroll invitations is a great way to invite all the guests on your list, and they have all the information they need to know.

To:

Write the name of your guest.

Where:

Provide the address for the party.

Greetings

To:

Where:

When:

Dress code:

RSVP.

When:

Include the time and date of the party.

Dress code:

Suggest what people should wear to your party.

RSVP:

Ask people to let you know if they can come.

MEDIEVAL MADNESS

These party games might not be traditional, but they are fun to make and play. Each one of these games has simple instructions to follow and can be personalized by using different colors, patterns, and designs.

GRAB THE FLAGS

Flags and banners decorated the great halls of royal castles. They would hang from the walls and ceiling, and each hall or castle had their own image called a coat of arms. These symbols were unique to one family, so you always knew whose house you were in.

You Will Need:

- PAPER • SCISSORS
- COLORED MARKERS

1. Fold a rectangular piece of paper in half.

2. Cut a "V" shape into the opposite end from the fold.

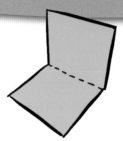

HOW TO PLAY

Hide the flags around the room. Race against other players or teams to collect all the flags of the same color. The fastest team or player wins.

3. Draw your coat of arms picture onto the front. Repeat until you have five identical flags.

4. Make a set of flags in different colors for each player or for the number of teams you have.

FACE THE FOOLS

Court jesters were good at acrobatics, juggling, telling jokes, and doing magic tricks. They were always doing their best to make people smile. Challenge your pals to a competition and try not to laugh as you pull the silliest faces. This game is sure to turn frowns upside down.

You Will Need:
- SCISSORS • GLUE STICK
- TAPE • COLORED MARKERS
- CONSTRUCTION PAPER • CARDBOARD
- CARDSTOCK (OR PAPER PLATE)

1. Cut out a circle of cardstock or use a paper plate. Draw a face onto the circle using markers.

2. Make a hat, collar, and circle bells using construction paper or cardstock.

3. Cut out a handle using some thick cardboard. Decorate by drawing on some diamond shapes.

4. Stick all the pieces together to make the mask. Repeat the steps so that everyone can have their own.

HOW TO PLAY

Two people play this game at a time and sit opposite each other. Both players hold up a mask so it covers their face. They make a silly face behind it and on the count of three reveal their face. The first to laugh loses the game and the winner goes on to challenge the next person.

CHAINED UP

Medieval shackles were used in dungeons to keep prisoners locked up if they had committed crimes. They were made from steel, so they were heavy to wear and almost impossible to escape from.

You Will Need:

- RUBBER BANDS • PAPER
- STAPLER • RULER
- PENCIL • SCISSORS

1. Cut up five small strips of paper that are 6 inches long and 2 inches wide.

2. Thread one piece of paper through a rubber band and staple into a circle. Repeat so you have two.

3. Join the two paper circles with more strips of paper stapled into circles.

4. Repeat so that you have enough for the number of people playing. Each person playing will need one chain.

HOW TO PLAY

Stand in a small circle. Each person puts a chain onto their right hand and reaches into the middle. Everyone puts their left hand through the other end of the chain of someone that is standing opposite. The goal of the game is to untangle everyone so that you are all standing in a circle without removing or breaking the chains.

JOUSTING TOURNAMENT

You Will Need:
- NEWSPAPER • GLUE STICK
- SCISSORS • CARDBOARD
- PAPER CUPS • PAINT
- PAINTBRUSH

Medieval jousting was a popular test of skill and courage. People wearing armor rode horses toward each other with long spears called lances and tried to be the first to hit the other.

1. Open up a piece of newspaper and spread some glue onto two edges. Roll the unglued side into a tight tube until you reach the opposite edge.

2. Open up another piece of newspaper and spread some glue on two edges. Roll up the original tube inside the newspaper to make a fatter tube. Repeat three or four times for each lance.

3. Cut out a circle from some thick cardboard. Cut a hole in the middle of the circle so it slides up the lance.

4. Make the targets by sticking cardboard rings onto upside down paper cups.

5. Decorate the targets and the lances with paint.

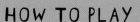

HOW TO PLAY
Place each of the targets on a table or chair. The two players stand about ten steps back facing their target. At the count of three, the players run toward the targets. The winner is the fastest to catch the target and hook it onto their lance.

PARTY DECORATIONS

Transform your home into a fort filled with decorations inspired by medieval times. Cover walls and tables, or hang them from the ceiling to give your party space a makeover, ready for your castle-themed celebrations.

COAT OF ARMS

A knight's armor covered his whole body, including his face, so it was hard to tell who was who. A coat of arms was designed for each knight with different pictures, words, and symbols so that each one was unique. This would be worn over the armor like a badge (or coat) and also on their flags and banners.

You Will Need:
- PAPER • PENCIL • SCISSORS
- OLD T-SHIRT • WOODEN STICK
- STRING • MARKERS

1. Draw a design onto a piece of paper. Try to include some animals, a shield, and a banner.

2. Cut out each element carefully so that you can use them as templates to draw around.

TOP TIP

With an adult, search the internet to see if your last name has a coat of arms linked to it. You could use this as inspiration for your design.

3. Fold the T-shirt in half and cut two lines to make the flag shape.

4. Use the paper templates to draw the design onto the fabric using markers.

5. Thread a wooden stick through the sleeves and tie string or ribbon onto the sides so it can be hung up.

FLYING DRAGONS

Tales of fierce dragons guarding precious treasures were popular in medieval times and often appeared in artwork. One of the most popular tales of the Middle Ages was about **Saint George and the Dragon. He rescued a princess from a dragon and saved a whole town.**

You Will Need:

- 2 PLASTIC MILK CARTONS • GREEN TISSUE PAPER OR MAGAZINE PAGES
- WHITE CRAFT GLUE • PAPER • PENCIL
- SCISSORS • PAINT • PAINTBRUSH

1. Tape together two plastic milk cartons.

2. Tear up pieces of green tissue paper or magazine pages and glue them onto the cartons. Let dry.

Why was King Arthur's army too tired to fight?

Because they had a few sleepless knights!

3. Cut out ears, eyes, wings, legs, a tail, and scales from colored paper.

4. Paint a nose, mouth, and scales.

5. Stick the cut-out paper to the body using more craft glue.

TOP TIP

Make the dragon soar through the air by tying string to the body and hanging it up.

17

TOURNAMENT TENTS

Knights would sleep in tents during their long expeditions or at events like jousting tournaments. They were often round, very colorful, and had flags and decorations hanging from them.

You Will Need:
- PAPER • MARKERS • PENCIL
- SCISSORS • TAPE

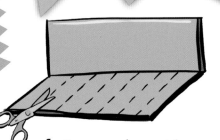

1. Cut out a long strip of paper (about half the size of a piece of paper) and fold it into six equal pieces.

2. Draw three quarters of a circle onto a piece of paper. Draw triangles all around the edge and cut it out.

3. Fold the circle together to make a cone. Color in the cone and paper strip using markers.

4. Stick the paper strip together to make a hexagon shape. Glue the cone to the top to make the roof.

5. Cut a slit halfway up one of the hexagon sides to make the opening of the tent and add some more flags to the outside.

TOP TIP
Make lots of these tents in different colors and use them to decorate your banquet table. You can make them in different sizes too!

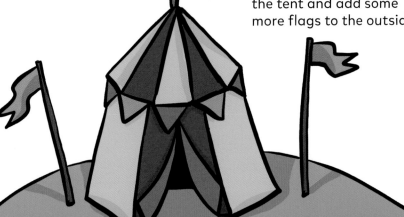

CASTLE AND DRAWBRIDGE

Medieval castles were built with tall, strong walls and were often surrounded by water to keep enemies out. When the drawbridge was up it was used as a big door to seal off the entrance, but when it was lowered it was used as a bridge so that you could cross the water.

1. Tape down the lids of four soda cans. Cover in paper and draw on some windows and bricks.

2. Cut squares out from the top of the cardboard box and decorate the outside with windows and bricks.

3. Cut the same size squares from the tops of four strips of cardboard and stick these onto the tops of the cans.

4. Make the door by cutting a rectangle from one side of the cardboard box. Then cut off all four corners.

5. Make a drawbridge from more cardboard and use string to attach it to the castle. Stick the turrets into the corners.

FANTASTIC FEASTS

Entertaining guests at banquets was a common medieval pastime. Tasty food was presented in a fancy way on a large table for the most important people. Impress your guests with these delicious recipes.

CASTLE TOWERS

Castle towers were often round so that you could see out in all directions and spot enemies approaching. They had small windows so that archers could fire arrows but also be protected from any incoming attacks.

You Will Need:
- PAPER • CARDBOARD BOX
- TAPE • SCISSORS
- COOKED POPCORN
- MARKERS

1. Wrap some paper loosely around a cardboard box and tape in place.

2. Fold one end as if you were wrapping a present and tape it down.

TOP TIP

Try making mint chocolate chip flavored popcorn! Mix a spoonful of honey with some mint extract and dark chocolate chips in a big bowl. Add the popcorn and coat evenly before serving.

3. Remove the box so you end up with a paper bag.

4. Cut out squares from the top and decorate to look like a tower.

5. Fill with popcorn and serve.

FLAMING TORCHES

Since the lightbulb was not invented until 1879, homes during the Middle Ages were lit by candlelight and fires. Torches were often used in castles, either mounted along the walls or held by hand to light the way.

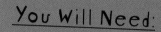

You Will Need:
- VANILLA ICE CREAM • ICE CREAM CONE
- MANGO • PINEAPPLE • KNIFE
- STRAWBERRY • WHITE CHOCOLATE
- ORANGE FOOD COLORING

1. With an adult, cut up some mango and pineapple slices into triangles.

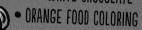

2. Mix together white chocolate and some orange food coloring.

3. Put a scoop of vanilla ice cream into an ice cream cone.

4. Drizzle the orange chocolate over the top.

5. Stick a strawberry into the middle of the ice cream and put the mango and pineapple slices around it.

FLAG COOKIES

This is a great activity to get your friends involved with the celebrations. Everyone gets a cookie to decorate and makes their own design. Use this project as a starting point and let your imagination do the rest.

You Will Need:

- COOKIES • CANDY
- ICING PENS
- FOOD COLORING
- PARCHMENT PAPER • MARKER

1. Draw a flag outline using icing pens.

2. Use different colored icing to fill in the shapes.

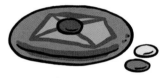

3. Press some candy into the middle and leave to set for a few minutes.

4. Draw the rest of the patterns onto the top using the icing pens.

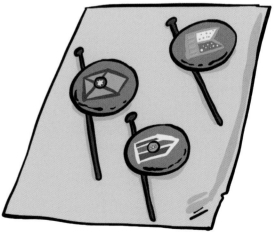

5. Display them on a sheet of parchment paper with flagpoles drawn on.

Why did St. George sleep during the day?
Because he went to knight school!

SAVORY AXES

Battle axes were popular weapons before being replaced by gunpowder in the 16th century. They were mostly made of iron or steel with a wooden handle and crafted by hand by the local blacksmith.

You Will Need:

- PUFF PASTRY • ROLLING PIN
- TIN FOIL • KNIFE • PAPER
- SCISSORS • PENCIL • TOMATO SAUCE
- PEPPERS • CHEESE • PRETZEL RODS

1. Fold a piece of paper in half and draw on a simple axe shape. Cut it out.

2. Roll out the ready-made puff pasty so that it is about ½ inch thick.

3. Use the template to cut out an axe head shape from the pastry.

20 MINUTES

4. Cover one half of the axe head with a layer of tomato sauce, chopped peppers, and cheese. Place a pretzel rod in the middle and fold over the other half.

5. Press down the edges so that the mixture is sealed in and bake for 20 minutes at a medium heat.

TOP TIP
Cover the pretzel rod handle in tin foil before you bake it so that it does not burn.

TINY TREASURES

Gather all your junk and transform it into toys, gifts, and prizes. Invite your friends over for a crafting party and ask them to bring any spare materials they have too.

CASTLE CASH

Bartering was a popular way to get the things you wanted by exchanging one thing for another. But as towns and villages grew, people used coins as a way to buy things. You would mostly find silver coins in medieval times, with gold only appearing later.

You Will Need:
- 1 CUP OF SALT • 2 CUPS OF FLOUR
- ¾ CUP WATER • SILVER PAINT
- PAINTBRUSH • CARDBOARD
- SCISSORS • PENCIL • WHITE CRAFT GLUE • PERMANENT MARKER

1. Cut out a circle of cardboard and decorate with pieces of cut cardboard to make a stamp.

2. Mix the salt, flour, and water together to make the dough. Add more water or flour if necessary.

3. Roll small amounts into balls and press them flat using the cardboard stamp.

1 HOUR

4. Bake at a low heat for about an hour or until they have dried out completely.

5. Paint the coins silver and leave to dry before adding any extra details with a permanent marker.

TOP TIP
Make a coin pouch by cutting out a circle of fabric and punching holes around the edge. Thread some ribbon through the holes and gather together to make the pouch.

CATAPULT

During medieval times, catapults were large wooden weapons that threw heavy objects, arrows, or stones great distances. As defenses grew better over the years, the catapult became less useful in battles.

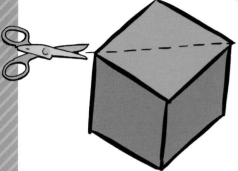

1. Cut the cardboard box in half so you have a triangle base.

2. Cut a wide slit up one side and make holes with a pencil at the top and the bottom of the triangle.

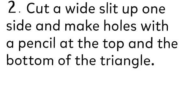

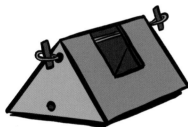

3. Thread a rubber band through the top two holes and keep it tight by holding it in place with a piece of cardboard on each side.

4. Put a pencil through the bottom two holes and tape a plastic spoon to the middle.

5. Keep the spoon upright by putting it in between the two sides of the rubber band.

HOW TO PLAY

Pull the spoon back, place some scrunched-up paper on the spoon, and let go to launch.

SWORD IN THE STONE

The Sword in the Stone is one of many stories about King Arthur. People from far and wide came to try and remove the magical sword that was stuck in the stone. Everyone failed except a young boy called Arthur, who was then crowned King of England.

1. Cut out a sword shape from cardboard.

You Will Need:
- CARDBOARD • TIN FOIL • GLUE STICK • TAPE
- NEWSPAPER • ACRYLIC PAINT • PAINTBRUSH

2. Wrap tin foil around the top to make it silver and mold more around the bottom to make the handle 3D.

3. Scrunch up a ball of newspaper around the tip of the sword and tape the ball together.

4. Remove the sword and wrap more foil around the ball of newspaper, keeping a gap for the sword to go in.

5. Paint the stone and the sword handle with paint.

DID YOU KNOW?
The Lady of the Lake is an alternative story about how King Arthur came to own his sword, Excalibur. In this story, King Arthur is given the sword by a mysterious and magical lady from a lake.

PHONE THRONE

Medieval royalty sat on large thrones made from wood with high backs and fancy decorations. They were positioned up high so that they would be seen as the most important person in the room.

You Will Need:
- CARDBOARD BOX (OLD MEDICINE BOTTLE PACKAGING IS PERFECT) • SCISSORS
- WHITE CRAFT GLUE • PAINT
- PAINTBRUSH • BLACK MARKER

1. Cut the box in half. Then cut the front and top off one of the halves.

2. Glue the part that was just cut so that it forms a seat. Stick this to the other half of the box with glue.

3. Decorate with paint. Use a black marker to add more details.

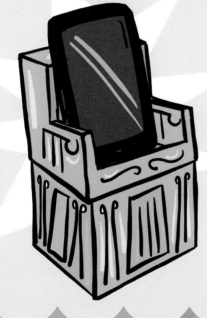

4. Cut a square of fabric and place it on the seat of the throne.

MINI KNIGHTS

These knights are a great way to recycle any soda cans left over from a party. You can also make them at a party with your friends! Line them up to play a bowling game, hide them around the house and try to find them, or see how many you can stack up before they all fall down.

You Will Need:
- SODA CANS • TIN FOIL • WHITE CRAFT GLUE • SCISSORS • CARDSTOCK
- CONSTRUCTION PAPER • TAPE

1. Tape down the lid of the can. Cover the middle of the can with a strip of tin foil.

2. Cut out two arms, a semi circle, and a sword from the cardstock.

3. Cover these with tin foil too.

4. Make a colorful shield from the construction paper and glue it to the middle of the can.

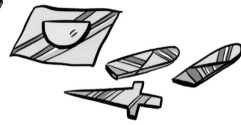

5. Cut out a face from the paper and stick it to the can along with the other silver pieces.

JOUSTING PENCIL TOPPER

As well as being a popular sport, jousting was sometimes used to determine if someone was guilty of a crime. A knight that won a jousting competition or tournament would be declared not guilty.

You Will Need:
- PENCIL • PAPER • SCISSORS
- COLORED MARKERS • GLUE STICK

1. Fold a piece of paper in half and make two small slits into the folded edge.

2. Open this up and draw a horse shape. Cut the horse out.

3. Fold another piece of paper in half and draw a knight.

4. Cut this out, remembering to cut slits for the arms.

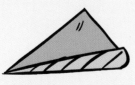

5. Roll up another piece of paper for the lance.

6. Stick the paper horse and the knight onto the pencil. Stick the lance under the arm.

Which knight likes to jump out and scare people?
Sir Prize!

JUGGLING BALLS

Medieval jugglers would earn their money by performing for people at fairs and market squares. Unlike the jesters at court, who were only employed by the king or the rich, these jugglers were like street performers and would entertain anyone that passed by.

You Will Need:
- BALLOONS • SCRAP PAPER • TAPE
- SCISSORS • SCRAP FELT OR FABRIC
- SAND OR RICE • WHITE CRAFT GLUE

3. Knot the open end of the balloon so that it won't leak.

1. Roll the piece of paper into a cone, taping it in place before cutting off the pointed end.

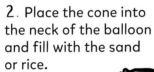

2. Place the cone into the neck of the balloon and fill with the sand or rice.

4. Draw and cut out the face and clothes from scrap felt or fabric.

5. Stick the fabric decorations onto the balloon using the white craft glue. Make several. Leave them to dry completely before using them to juggle.

TOP TIP
Its easiest to learn to juggle with three balls, and it's a good idea to make them all the same size.

ROYAL PUPPETS

The medieval period lasted hundreds of years. There were many different leaders during that time. Strict rules meant that all those who ruled were male. Empress Matilda was the only living child of the English king in 1135, but her male cousin, Stephen of Blois, was chosen to rule England instead.

1. Stuff some scrap fabric into the top of the sock and then place the stick inside the sock.

2. Secure the scrap fabric in place with a rubber band so it makes a ball.

You Will Need:
- SOCK • SCRAP FABRIC
- RUBBER BANDS • SCISSORS
- PAPER CUP • WOODEN STICK OR SKEWER • FABRIC GLUE

3. Make a hole in the middle of the paper cup and put the stick through it.

4. Place the sock around the edge of the cup and hold it in place using another rubber band.

5. Decorate the puppet with scrap fabric. Make a face, hair, arms, clothes, and a crown.

KNIGHTS PUZZLE

CAN YOU FIND THE ANSWERS TO THESE QUESTIONS?

1. Which knight does not have a belt buckle?

2. How many flags can you count in the picture?

3. Which knight has a different weapon than the others?

4. Can you spot which knight has different shoes?

ANSWERS 1.B 2. 8 flags 3.A 4.C